WHERE'S JESS?

By Joy and Marv Johnson
with The Goldsteins—Heather, Ray, and Jody
artwork by Shari Barum

I asked Mommy and Daddy, "Where's Jess?"
They told me Jess is dead.

I want to know what dead is.

Is dead like sleeping?

Mommy said dead was not like sleeping.

Is dead like going on a trip?

Daddy said dead was not like going on a trip.

Mommy says dead means Jess doesn't breathe in or out now. All the parts in Jess' body stopped working.

Daddy says dead means Jess doesn't think or feel anymore. He says Jess won't come home.

Jess is in a special place for dead people.

Mommy and Daddy say we won't see Jess anymore.
I see Jess' toys and Jess' Teddy.
I see pictures of Jess on our walls and in our books.
Sometimes when I sleep I dream of Jess, too.

I can remember Jess.

And sometimes when we rock together, Daddy cries. Daddy says he's thinking about Jess.

Daddy remembers Jess, too.

Sometimes when I talk about Jess, Mommy cries.
I'm scared that my talking makes her cry.
Mommy smiles. She says I don't need to be afraid of her tears.

I can talk about Jess all I want to.

One time I hurt my knee and cried.
Mommy says when someone we love dies
we hurt way deep down inside.

She says crying can help us feel better.

Sometimes I think maybe I did something bad
and that is why Jess is dead.
Daddy and Mommy say "No."
Nothing I did or thought made Jess die.

It wasn't because of me.

I play in my playroom.
I used to call it Jess' room.
After Jess died they took away Jess' bed.
They took away Jess' room.

I miss Jess.

Mommy says we will all miss Jess for a long time.
We say, remember when . . . and we talk about Jess.
We laugh sometimes, too.

I know Mommy and Daddy love me. I'm OK.